Boys Will Be Boys

Celebrating *the* Adventurous Spirit in Every Little Boy

paintings by
Jim Daly

HARVEST HOUSE PUBLISHERS

EUGENE, OREGON

Boys Will Be Boys
Copyright © 2004 by Jim Daly
Published by Harvest House Publishers
Eugene, Oregon 97402

ISBN 0-7369-1312-2

Artwork copyright © Jim Daly and may not be reproduced without permission. For more information
regarding art prints featured in this book, please contact:

    Jim Daly
    P.O. Box 25146
    Eugene, OR 97402
    Email: caroledaly@comcast.net

Design and production by Koechel Peterson & Associates, Inc., Minneapolis, Minnesota

Harvest House Publishers has made every effort to trace the ownership of all poems and quotes.
In the event of a question arising from the use of a poem or quote, we regret any error made and
will be pleased to make the necessary correction in future editions of this book.

Scripture quotations are taken from the HOLY BIBLE, NEW INTERNATIONAL VERSION®
NIV®. Copyright©1973, 1978, 1984 by the International Bible Society. Used by permission of
Zondervan. All rights reserved.

Printed in China

04 05 06 07 08 09 10 / IM / 10 9 8 7 6 5 4 3 2

THERE COMES A TIME
in every rightly constructed boy's life
when he has a raging desire to go
somewhere and dig for hidden treasure.

MARK TWAIN

WHEN I AM GROWN TO MAN'S ESTATE
I shall be very proud and great,
And tell the other girls and boys
Not to meddle with my toys.

ROBERT LOUIS STEVENSON

BOYS ARE BEYOND
the range of anybody's
sure understanding, at least
when they are between the ages
of 18 months and 90 years.

JAMES THURBER

Secret Spot

First Meeting

BUT THE BOYS GREW BIG AND BOLDER—

one, a sturdy, brown-faced lad,
With his axe upon his shoulder, loved to go to work "like dad,"
And another in the saddle took a bush-bred native's pride,
And he boasted he could straddle any nag his dad could ride.

EDWARD DYSON

A FAIRLY BRIGHT BOY

is far more intelligent
and far better company
than the average adult.

JOHN B. S. HALDANE

Stand Off

"She won't stay long then, if I can help it," muttered Tom, who regarded girls as a very unnecessary portion of creation. Boys of fourteen are apt to think so, and perhaps it is a wise arrangement; for, being fond of turning somersaults, they have an opportunity of indulging in a good one, metaphorically speaking, when, three or four years later, they become the abject slaves of "those bothering girls."

LOUISA MAY ALCOTT
An Old-Fashioned Girl

EACH CHILD IS AN ADVENTURE

into a better life — an opportunity to change the old pattern and make it new.

HUBERT H. HUMPHREY

BE HAPPY, YOUNG MAN,

while you are young, and let your heart give you joy in the days of your youth. Follow the ways of your heart…

THE BOOK OF ECCLESIASTES

"Mr. Chairman and boys. You all know what has brought us together. We want to start a club for playing baseball, like the big clubs they have in Brooklyn and New York."

"How shall we do it?" asked Henry Scott.

"We must first appoint a captain of the club, who will have power to assign the members to their different positions. Of course you will want one that understands about these matters."

"He means himself," whispered Henry Scott, to his next neighbor; and here he was right...

"Boys," he announced, amid a universal stillness, "there is one vote for Sam Pomeroy, one for Eugene Morton, and the rest are for Frank Fowler, who is elected."

There was a clapping of hands, in which Tom Pinkerton did not join.

Frank Fowler, who is to be our hero, came forward a little, and spoke modestly as follows: "Boys, I thank you for electing me captain of the club. I am afraid I am not very well qualified for the place, but I will do as well as I can."

HORATIO ALGER
The Cash Boy

IT'S FUN BEING A KID.

BRADFORD A. ANGLER

Tush! tush! fear boys with bugs.

WILLIAM SHAKESPEARE

Odd Man Out

"Clear the lulla!" was the general cry on a bright December afternoon, when all the boys and girls of Harmony Village were out enjoying the first good snow of the season. Up and down three long coasts they went as fast as legs and sleds could carry them. One smooth path led into the meadow, and here the little folk congregated; one swept across the pond, where skaters were darting about like water-bugs; and the third, from the very top of the steep hill, ended abruptly at a rail fence on the high bank above the road. There was a group of lads and lasses sitting or leaning on this fence to rest after an exciting race, and, as they reposed, they amused themselves with criticising their mates, still absorbed in this most delightful of outdoor sports.

LOUISA MAY ALCOTT
Jack and Jill

CHILDREN ARE REMARKABLE

for their intelligence and ardor,
for their curiosity, their intolerance
of shams, the clarity and
ruthlessness of their vision.

ALDOUS HUXLEY

Children are the living messages
we send to a time we will not see.

JOHN W. WHITEHEAD

Close Inspection

Storytime

JEFFREY IS NOT A BAD OR REBELLIOUS KID.

He's just a boy. And in case you haven't noticed, boys are different than girls…Haven't you heard your parents or grandparents say with a smile, "Girls are made out of sugar and spice and everything nice, but boys are made of snakes and snails and puppy-dog tails"? It was said tongue-in-cheek, but people of all ages thought it was based on fact. "Boys will be boys," they said knowingly. They were right.

DR. JAMES DOBSON
Bringing Up Boys

BUT IT SO HAPPENED THAT NATURE

had given to the youngest son gifts which she had not bestowed upon his elder brothers. He had a beautiful face and a fine, strong, graceful figure; he had a bright smile and a sweet, gay voice; he was brave and generous, and had the kindest heart in the world, and seemed to have the power to make every one love him.

FRANCES HODGES BURNETT
Little Lord Fauntleroy

He tried the luxury of doing good.

GEORGE CRABBE

IT WAS A VERY STRANGE THING INDEED.

She quite caught her breath as she stopped to look at it. A boy was sitting under a tree, with his back against it, playing on a rough wooden pipe. He was a funny looking boy about twelve. He looked very clean and his nose turned up and his cheeks were as red as poppies and never had Mistress Mary seen such round and such blue eyes in any boy's face. And on the trunk of the tree he leaned against, a brown squirrel was clinging and watching him, and from behind a bush nearby a cock pheasant was delicately stretching his neck to peep out, and quite near him were two rabbits sitting up and sniffing with tremulous noses—and actually it appeared as if they were all drawing near to watch him and listen to the strange low little call his pipe seemed to make.

When he saw Mary he held up his hand and spoke to her in a voice almost as low as and rather like his piping.

"Don't tha' move," he said. "It'd flight 'em." Mary remained motionless. He stopped playing his pipe and began to rise from the ground. He moved so slowly that it scarcely seemed as though he were moving at all, but at last he stood on his feet and then the squirrel scampered back up into the branches of his tree, the pheasant withdrew his head and the rabbits dropped on all fours and began to hop away, though not at all as if they were frightened.

"I'm Dickon," the boy said. "I know tha'rt Miss Mary."

Then Mary realized that somehow she had known at first that he was Dickon. Who else could have been charming rabbits and pheasants as the natives charm snakes in India? He had a wide, red, curving mouth and his smile spread all over his face.

FRANCES HODGES BURNETT
The Secret Garden

But there was such an influence in Mr. Wickfield's old house, that when I knocked at it, with my new school-books under my arm, I began to feel my uneasiness softening away. As I went up to my airy old room, the grave shadow of the staircase seemed to fall upon my doubts and fears, and to make the past more indistinct. I sat there, sturdily conning my books, until dinner-time (we were out of school for good at three); and went down, hopeful of becoming a passable sort of boy yet.

CHARLES DICKENS
David Copperfield

WE WERE BOYS TOGETHER,
And never can forget
In childhood where we met;
The school-house near the heather,
The humble home to memory dear,
Its sorrows and its joys;
Where woke the transient smile or tear,
When you and I were boys.

GEORGE POPE MORRIS

Worn Out

Lest the title should mislead the reader, I hasten to assure him here that I have no dark confessions to make. I call my story the story of a bad boy, partly to distinguish myself from those faultless young gentlemen who generally figure in narratives of this kind, and partly because I really was not a cherub. I may truthfully say I was an amiable, impulsive lad, blessed with fine digestive powers, and no hypocrite. I didn't want to be an angel and with the angels stand; I didn't think the missionary tracts presented to me by the Rev. Wibird Hawkins were half so nice as *Robinson Crusoe*; and I didn't send my little pocket-money to the natives of the Feejee Islands, but spent it royally in peppermint-drops and taffy candy. In short, I was a real human boy, such as you may meet anywhere in New England, and no more like the impossible boy in a storybook than a sound orange is like one that has been sucked dry.

THOMAS BAILEY ALDRICH
The Story of a Bad Boy

NATURE MAKES BOYS

and girls lovely to look upon
so they can be tolerated until
they acquire some sense.

WILLIAM LYON PHELPS

"Have you lived for some time in the city?"

"No; I came here only yesterday from the country."

"I think country boys are very foolish to leave good homes in the country to seek places in the city," said Mrs. Pitkin sharply.

"There may be circumstances, Lavinia, that make it advisable," suggested Mr. Carter, who, however, did not know Phil's reason for coming.

"No doubt; I understand that," answered Mrs. Pitkin, in a tone so significant that Phil wondered whether she thought he had got into any trouble at home.

"And besides, we can't judge for every one. So I hope Master Philip may find some good and satisfactory opening, now that he has reached the city."

HORATIO ALGER
The Errand Boy

A SCOUT SMILES
and whistles under
all circumstances.

ROBERT BADEN-POWELL

Chores First

On the Sunday after Christmas Claude and Ernest were walking along the banks of Lovely Creek. They had been as far as Mr. Wheeler's timber claim and back. It was like an autumn afternoon, so warm that they left their overcoats on the limb of a crooked elm by the pasture fence. The fields and the bare tree-tops seemed to be swimming in light. A few brown leaves still clung to the bushy trees along the creek. In the upper pasture, more than a mile from the house, the boys found a bittersweet vine that wound about a little dogwood and covered it with scarlet berries. It was like finding a Christmas tree growing wild out of doors.

WILLA CATHER
On Lovely Creek

Where the pools are bright and deep,
Where the grey trout lies asleep,
Up the river and over the lea,
That's the way for Billy and me.

Why the boys should drive away
Little sweet maidens from the play,
Or love to banter and fight so well,
That's the thing I never could tell.

But this I know, I love to play
Through the meadow, among the hay;
Up the water and over the lea,
That's the way for Billy and me.

JAMES HOGG
"A Boy's Song"

GOD'S LITTLE BOY

makes friends with others;
Those friends include his
sisters and brothers.
True friends are always
a gift from above;
Make it your goal to
give brotherly love.

JIM AND ELIZABETH GEORGE

THERE WAS NEVER A CHILD

so lovely but his mother was
glad to get him to sleep.

RALPH WALDO EMERSON

Jack tried to laugh, but it was rather a failure, though he managed to say, cheerfully, "That was good of old Joe. I wouldn't lend him Thunderbolt for fear he'd hurt it. Couldn't have smashed it up better than I did, could he? Don't think I want any pieces to remind me of that fall. I just wish you'd seen us, Mother! It must have been a splendid spill to look at, anyway."

LOUISA MAY ALCOTT
Jack and Jill

Far off he heard the city's hum and noise,
And now and then the shriller laughter where
The passionate purity of brown-limbed boys
Wrestled or raced in the clear healthful air,
And now and then a little tinkling bell
As the shorn wether led the sheep
down to the mossy well.

OSCAR WILDE

A Timeless Summer

Emil was quite different, being quick-tempered, restless, and enterprising, bent on going to sea, for the blood of the old Vikings stirred in his veins, and could not be tamed. His uncle promised that he should go when he was sixteen, and set him to studying navigation, gave him stories of good and famous admirals and heroes to read, and let him lead the life of a frog in river, pond, and brook, when lessons were done. His room looked like the cabin of a man-of-war, for every thing was nautical, military, and shipshape. Captain Kyd was his delight, and his favorite amusement was to rig up like that piratical gentleman, and roar out sanguinary sea-songs at the top of his voice. He would dance nothing but sailors' hornpipes, rolled in his gait, and was as nautical in conversation to his uncle as he would permit. The boys called him "Commodore," and took great pride in his fleet, which whitened the pond and suffered disasters that would have daunted any commander but a sea-struck boy.

LOUISA MAY ALCOTT
Little Men

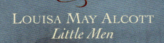

PRETTY MUCH ALL THE HONEST
truth telling there is in the world
is done by children.

AUTHOR UNKNOWN

The Coach

THE NINTH RECKONED OTHERWISE;

he opened a little account with God in which he placed upon the one side as Debit: "He will allow me to pass," and on the other side as Credit: "I will never tell any more lies, nor gossip, will always go to church, let the girls alone, and break myself of swearing." But the tenth thought that as Ole Hansen had passed last year, it would be worse than injustice if he did not pass this year, for he had always been above him at school, and besides, his parents were not respectable.

BJÖRNSTJERNE BJÖRNSON
A Happy Boy

THE LITTLE BOYS

of Harbury when they
are laid to sleep,
Dream of masts and cabins
and the wonders
of the deep.

LOUISE DRISCOLL

I remember, when quite a small boy, building an immense man kite, seven-feet high. It was a gorgeous affair, with its brilliant red nose and cheeks, blue coat, and striped trousers…My man flew splendidly; he required no running, no hoisting, no jerking of the string to assist him. I had only to stand on the high bank and let out the string, and so fast did the twine pass through my hands that my fingers were almost blistered.

Daniel Carter Beard
The American Boy's Handy Book

For cider, after school, in late September?
Or gather hazel nuts among the thickets
On Aaron Hatfield's farm when the frosts begin?
For many times with the laughing girls and boys
Played I along the road and over the hills
When the sun was low and the air was cool,
Stopping to club the walnut tree
Standing leafless against a flaming west.

EDGAR LEE MASTERS

WE TWO BOYS TOGETHER CLINGING,
One the other never leaving,
Up and down the roads going—
North and South excursions making,
Power enjoying—elbows stretching—fingers clutching,
Arm'd and fearless—eating, drinking, sleeping…

WALT WHITMAN

WE WORRY ABOUT WHAT A CHILD
will become tomorrow,
yet we forget that he
is someone today.

STACIA TAUSCHER

There was a great clashing of tin pails, much running to and fro, and frequent demands for something to eat, one August afternoon, for the boys were going huckleberrying, and made as much stir about it as if they were setting out to find the North West Passage.

LOUISA MAY ALCOTT
Little Men

THERE'S NOTHING THAT CAN

help you understand
your beliefs more than
trying to explain them to an
inquisitive child.

FRANK A. CLARK

You are worried about seeing him spend his early years in doing nothing. What! Is it nothing to be happy? Nothing to skip, play, and run around all day long? Never in his life will he be so busy again.

JEAN-JACQUES ROUSSEAU

WHEN ONE ASKED HIM

what boys should learn, "That," said he, "which they shall use when men."

PLUTARCH

Almanzo's long brown pants buttoned to his red waist with a row of bright brass buttons, all around his middle. The waist's collar buttoned snuggly up to his chin, and so did his long coat of brown fullcloth. Mother had made his cap of the same brown fullcloth, with cozy ear-flaps that tied under his chin. And his red mittens were on a string that went up the sleeves of his coat and across the back of his neck. That was so he couldn't lose them.

LAURA INGALLS WILDER
Farmer Boy

You can learn many things from
children. How much patience
you have, for instance.

FRANKLIN P. JONES

THERE ARE NO SEVEN WONDERS
of the world in the eyes of a child.
There are seven million.

WALT STREIGHTIFF

ONE OF THE MOST OBVIOUS FACTS
about grownups to a child is
that they have forgotten what
it is like to be a child.

RANDALL JARRELL